it was thirty years ago today

TERENCE SPENCER

BLOOMSBURY

First published in Great Britain 1994
This paperback edition published 1995
Bloomsbury Publishing Limited, 2 Soho Square, London W1V 5DE

Photographs copyright © 1994 by Bloomsbury Publishing Ltd
Text copyright © 1994 by Terence Spencer
Design copyright © 1994 by Bloomsbury Publishing Ltd

The moral right of the author has been asserted

A CIP catalogue record for this book is available
from the British Library

ISBN 0-7475-22383

10 9 8 7 6 5 4 3 2 1

Printed in Italy by Artegrafica

Designed by
BRADBURY AND WILLIAMS

Prints from Terence Spencer's negatives: Ron Bagley
Retouching: Jayne Wiltshire

CONTENTS

BEATLES? WHAT BEATLES?

Towards the end of 1963 I returned to England after covering stories on trouble spots around the world for the American magazine *Life*. The moment we met at the airport my daughter Cara, then aged thirteen, said to me, 'Dad, Dad, you've got to do a story on those fab Beatles!' As I'd never heard of them my reaction was pretty much, 'Oh God, what's she on about now?' and I think I looked down at the ground to see if something was crawling around my feet.

But when I arrived at the office next morning I found that everyone was talking about this great new group which was apparently setting new trends, not only musically but culturally — at least as far as the young were concerned. They had already had one Number 2 and two Number 1 hits in 1963, and the record that was to become their third Number 1, 'I Wanna Hold Your Hand', had sold a million copies before its release in November. Yet they were virtually unknown outside the UK. So when we suggested to our New York office that we might do a story on them, the reaction was cool, to say the least.

Nevertheless, a colleague and I decided to go along to the Prince of Wales Theatre — where the Beatles were appearing in the Royal Variety Performance on 4 November — just to see what all the fuss was about. From the moment we arrived we could tell that this was like nothing we had ever seen before. There were mobs of screaming teenage girls outside the theatre, and when the Beatles came on stage you could hardly hear what they were playing because the audience's screaming was so deafening. It used to come in waves. When the boys did one of their high 'Oooooooooh' bits, the girls just went mad . . .

That was the night John Lennon asked those in the cheap seats to clap and the others to 'rattle yer jewellery'. The Royals obviously loved the whole thing. In fact, they were probably the only ones who could hear the music — everyone else was screaming so loudly.

Once we had seen the Beatles on stage, we knew we had to do a story on them. They were due to play at the Winter Gardens in Bournemouth on 16 November: so Frank Allen, our office driver and photographer's assistant, and I set off on their trail. Normally we would have approached the manager and made arrangements, but for some reason we didn't this time. We simply decided to take our cameras and try our luck.

We knew the Beatles would be staying in an out-of-the-way place to avoid the more hysterical of their fans. By this time they were sufficiently widely recognised to have begun to feel like prisoners: their girl fans went so wild at the sight of them that they couldn't let themselves be seen outside a theatre or in the street for their own physical safety.

Frank, who doesn't know the meaning of the word 'no', tracked them down at the elegant Branksome Towers Hotel, outside Bournemouth. And so the strange association between a couple of middle-aged journalists and four legendary mop-tops began. Over the next few months we followed them around the country and over to Paris, shooting them on stage and off, and collecting a huge pile of fascinating photographs.

Cara listens to the Fab Four.
Note the Beatles haircut.

Because I worked with a number of cameras and sent my film unseen to New York, I had to keep accurate captions. In order to do this I carried a small tape-recorder and mike attached to my lapel. One night after a show when we were all fooling around in the backstage bar, I said to John, 'How about a message for my daughter, Cara, as it's because of her that I'm here?'

'Sure, sure,' said John, grabbing his guitar, and spoke into my mike: 'Hello, Cara. How are you? We have your old man here buggering us around, following us everywhere.' So the message went on, laden with expletives. He called to George, 'Say a few words to Terry's little girl.' George came over, harmonising his guitar with John's, and they were soon joined by the others, each saying a few words into the mike. They ad-libbed a short personal song to Cara, accompanied by their guitars, with Ringo beating out the rhythm on the bar.

This was a wonderful tape to have at the height of the Beatles' fame, but I was slightly worried about giving such an expletive-ridden present to my daughter. 'What are we going to do about it?' I asked my wife, Lesley.

'There's not one word in it she hasn't already heard from you,' was her reply.

So Cara took the tape and played it on the bus going to school. The conductress came to listen and no one paid their fares. At school the girls gathered furtively in the lavatory to listen to it. They were in raptures.

At the time I often used to plug my tape recorder into the telephone system to record messages from *Life*'s Paris office. One evening I failed to take the recorder out of the 'record' mode. Cara came back with a friend to play the tape for the umpteenth time, only to find that she had wiped it completely. It was a tragic day, with tears for many nights to come, though the fact that I was later able to introduce her to the boys themselves consoled her a little.

After the *Life* article was published, I saw the Beatles a few times and took some more of the photographs in this book, but there was nothing like the contact there had been over the previous months.

Then Paul married Linda Eastman in 1969 and settled down to family life in a remote part of Scotland. For some reason a rumour started that he was dead. *Life* wanted to prove that he wasn't. We tracked the farmhouse down and I went there with *Life* reporter Dorothy Bacon, arriving early on a Sunday morning when we knew that the farmers who guarded the McCartneys' privacy would be at church. As we surreptitiously approached the house, Paul emerged, scruffy, unshaven and carrying a bucket. I took a shot. At the click of the camera he looked up, turned red with rage and threw the bucket at me as I grabbed another shot. Then he rushed over and hit me across the right ear.

'Dorothy,' I shouted, 'I think we've proved that Paul is very much alive! Let's get the hell out of here – fast!'

As we retreated down the dirt road we saw Paul's Land-rover catching us up. For a nasty moment we thought he was going to try and run us down, but he stopped the car and got out, shaven and spruced. Linda was with him. He walked towards us with his hand out.

'I'm really sorry about this,' he said, 'and I want to make a deal with you. You give me that roll of film and we will give you a beautiful set of pictures that Linda has taken of us and the children up here in Scotland.'

I knew Linda was a professional photographer and I also knew that the couple of frames I had taken were not the sort of pictures *Life* wanted, but a photographer does not give away film. I have been arrested in the past for refusing to hand over film. But I understood how Paul felt and I trusted him to keep his word. We shook hands and did the deal.

You do not have to go to wars to meet trouble. In fact, in my long career the only person to have hit me was Paul McCartney. But it was worth it. *Life* proved that Paul McCartney was alive by using Linda's pictures.

That was the last occasion I met any of the Beatles. But the time I spent with them remains special to me. Although I was forty-five when I met them and they were in their early twenties, I was truly charmed by their charisma and their sound. Such numbers as 'She Loves You', 'Love Me Do' and 'I Wanna Hold Your Hand' haunt me to this day. These photographs are a happy reminder of those extraordinary times.

Terence Spencer, 1994

1

WITH THE BEATLES

The Beatles seemed to like Frank and me from the start, despite the fact that we were twice their age. That was lucky for us, because they were completely unimpressed by who we were. Normally we would have been welcomed because we worked for *Life* – its circulation was about six million in those days and showbiz people would do almost anything to get their name or picture in the magazine. But the Beatles had never heard of it and couldn't have cared less. Later Ringo remembered having seen a copy in his dentist's waiting-room. Nevertheless they took to us, invited us back stage at Bournemouth that first night and told us what their movements were the following morning.

I was always fascinated watching the Beatles prepare for a show. They were careful about their appearance, making sure their shirts were freshly laundered, their ties were straight and their hair immaculate, but none of them was in the least bit vain. They were happy for me to hang around, knowing that I wasn't going to intrude or take the sort of picture that some of the tabloids might want today. They didn't want to pose for shots, but that wasn't the kind of photograph I wanted, anyway. They always reacted well to my pictures, studying the contacts avidly and often asking me for prints. Even today I don't think there's a single one in my collection that would offend them, and I took about 5,000 pictures in all. Perhaps it was because we got on well together that I found them so photogenic – you'd have a job, anyway, to take a bad picture of the Beatles.

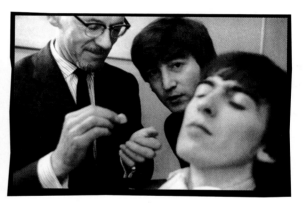

A STYLE IS BORN

Once they started performing professionally, the Beatles were quite self-conscious about their appearance. Thanks to the influence of their manager, Brian Epstein, they were impeccably groomed when they went on stage. They used to sit in front of a long mirror — they always shared a dressing-room — to do their hair and make themselves up.

MOP-TOPS

They used minimal make-up, just a little powder to offset the sweat from the strong stage lighting. Although long hair was considered anti-establishment in those days, the Beatles' mop-tops were always immaculately clean and carefully styled. They gave a lot of attention to their appearance, but they weren't at all conceited.

(Overleaf)
FINISHING TOUCHES

A last glance in the mirror, a quick comb through the hair, a final straightening of the collar and the Beatles are ready to face their fans.

PLAYING IT STRAIGHT

By this time the Beatles had a tailor, Doug Millings. Here Ringo, living up to his reputation as the group clown, refuses to take a fitting seriously.

READY TO GO

George takes a final swig of milk before going on stage. I never saw any of the boys display any nervousness before a show. It was all very relaxed. They really didn't realise what had hit them or understand the pressures that fame would eventually bring.

2

PASSING THE TIME

Fighting off boredom was always a problem with the Beatles. From the moment they became so popular that they had to hide from their fans, there was a lot of hanging around to do, a lot of time spent waiting in their dressing-room until they were due to go on stage. Finding ways of filling in those hours became almost an obsession.

They never handled money – Brian Epstein did that for them – and I doubt whether any of them had an idea of how much they were worth. Even if they had, they couldn't have gone out to the shops without being mobbed. If they wanted anything, they asked Neil Aspinall, their road manager, to get it for them. Brian and Neil pandered to them as if they were sick children, bringing them toys and games that might amuse them and stop them from becoming restless. They brought in electric trains and motor cars which all four would gleefully race against each other.

The fans also sent them presents – by the sackful. These would be waiting in the dressing-room before every show and the boys would make a rush for them the moment they arrived. If this was some hours before they were due to perform, as it often was, they would then play until it was time to prepare for the show.

Considering how much time they spent cooped up together, the Beatles seemed to get on well together. 'Of course we have rows,' John said, 'but they are never serious. We've been hanging around together for years as friends. Usually it's people who get together just for business who crack up.'

LIGHT RELIEF

All the Beatles smoked incessantly – I suppose it was one way of alleviating boredom. But I never smelled marijuana anywhere near them, and they mostly preferred tea or Pepsi to alcohol. Unlike the Rolling Stones, who cultivated a rebellious image, the Beatles gave the impression of wholesomeness in both their public and their private lives.

TWO MUSKETEERS

Anything to pass the time: George and Ringo fool around with fencing swords back stage.

A Scalextric model racing-car set went with the Beatles everywhere. They competed fiercely against each other and never seemed to tire of the game.

WITH LOVE FROM . . .

Keeping up with the constant demand for autographs was something else that kept the Beatles busy. In due course the job became too much for them, and roadies and others from the entourage had to sign some of the pictures that were sent out to fans. Years later, when Beatles autographs were fetching high prices at places like Sotheby's, experts had a hard time sifting out the fakes from the originals.

BLOW-UP

All my film, mostly Kodak Tri X, was sent to New York, where it was inspection-developed in the great Life *lab. Every time I got a batch of contact sheets back, I'd take them up and show the boys — they always wanted to see them and generally reacted enthusiastically. The sheet that Ringo is looking at here is reproduced opposite: the pictures show the Beatles receiving their first gold and silver discs.*

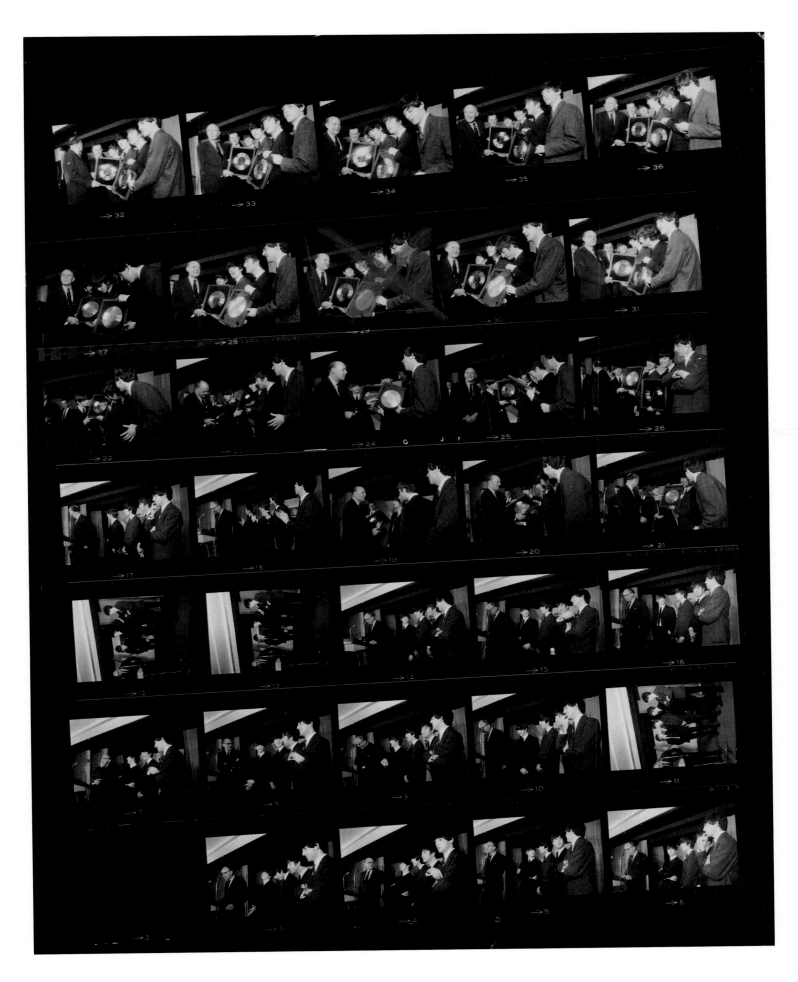

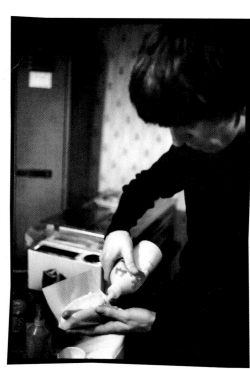

GLORIOUS FOOD

When they were doing their 1963 Christmas Show at the Astoria in Finsbury Park, North London, the Beatles still felt able to venture into the canteen. Later, food was brought to the dressing-room and there was often something with chips brought in before a performance.

TEATIME

Rolf Harris and the policeman on duty were among those who came into the dressing-room at the Astoria for a cuppa before the show.

EVERY PICTURE TELLS A STORY

Although Paul seems to be absorbed in my contacts here — and to have appropriated my camera — George and Ringo were the most interested in photography when I was with them. I was using four or five Nikon 35mm cameras and often left them lying around back stage. George and Ringo would pick them up and start snapping each other or their friends. They became fascinated with the cameras and I spent many hours teaching them all about Nikons — only to find that they had both gone out and bought Pentaxes!

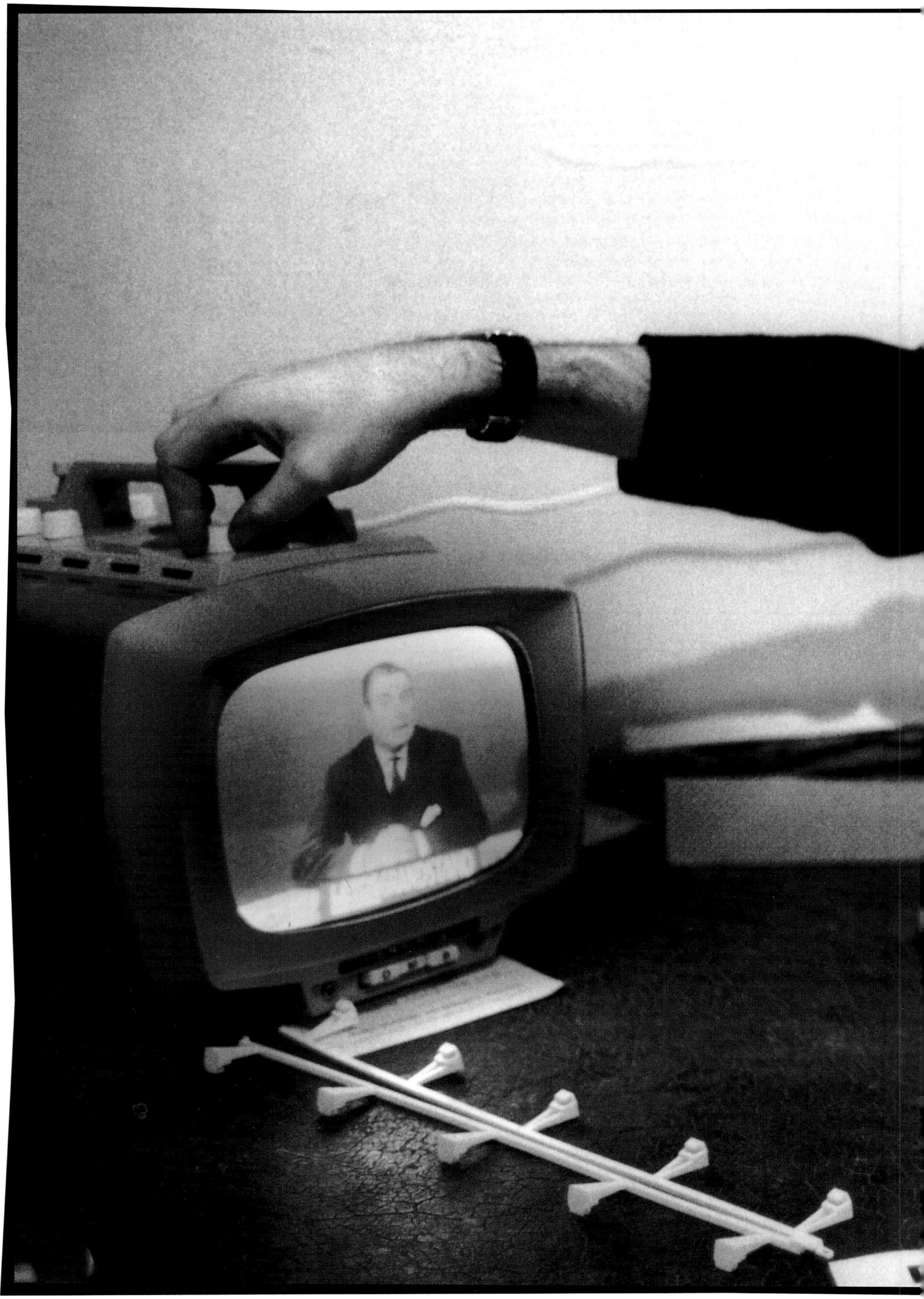

EDDIE WARING PRESENTS
Here Paul watches the late
Eddie Waring on television.

WITH A LITTLE HELP FROM
MY FRIENDS

Another way of alleviating the boredom was to have your mates round, and friends of the Beatles' often dropped into their dressing-room. Actress Sandra Caron (in the furry hat) was a great pal, as was her sister, the singer Alma Cogan; actress Fenella Fielding was another visitor.

The picture overleaf shows the Beatles chatting with Rolling Stone Mick Jagger. The Stones' first Top 20 hit 'I Wanna Be Your Man' was in the charts at the time (this was a Lennon and McCartney composition). Liverpool musician, Johnny Gustafson looks on.

3

TWIST AND SHOUT

On stage the Beatles seemed as calm and relaxed as they did in their dressing-room. As they walked on they would be greeted by rapturous screaming and frenzy, but appeared unconcerned. They talked and joked with each other and the audience.

They once announced publicly that they liked jelly babies. As a result, at their next concert the stage was bombarded with sweets which came flying through the air from all directions. John remarked, 'They are the most adhesive substance known to man. Sometimes the kids think we are trying out new dance steps, when all we are trying to do is to get our feet unstuck from the stage.' Crumpled messages also used to litter the stage.

It was a bit of a problem for me trying to shoot photographs from the front of the stage, because I had to force myself between the fans and the phalanx of policemen guarding the stage. One copper remarked, 'These girls are like eels, they slither through your legs in their crazed dash to get near the Beatles. They become totally oblivious to danger.'

Nothing was rational in those early Beatles days. The whole Beatles phenomenon was an extraordinary thing to be happening to four such young, ordinary lads. John was twenty-three at this time, Paul nearly two years younger. They had met in 1957 when Paul was recruited as guitarist to John's skiffle band, the Quarry Men. George was a year younger than Paul, but the two had known each other as children. It was Paul who introduced George to John, when George was only fourteen. So those three went back a long way together. Ringo was the oldest of the four and had known the others through the Liverpool rock 'n' roll circuit, but had only been recruited to the Beatles in August 1962, following the controversial sacking of their previous drummer, Pete Best.

OH, NO, YOU DON'T!

The Beatles Christmas Show at the Astoria ran from Christmas Eve 1963 to 11 January 1964 and included snatches of pantomime as well as 'straight' concert performances. The Times' 'serious' music critic William Mann, in an article published between Christmas and the New Year, described Lennon and McCartney as 'the outstanding English composers of 1963', referring to 'pandiatonic clusters' and 'an Aeolian cadence' in their music and attributing to them qualities which certainly would have surprised them. At the other end of the critical spectrum, comedienne Dora Bryan paid them the compliment of releasing 'All I Want for Christmas is a Beatle', which was the season's novelty hit record.

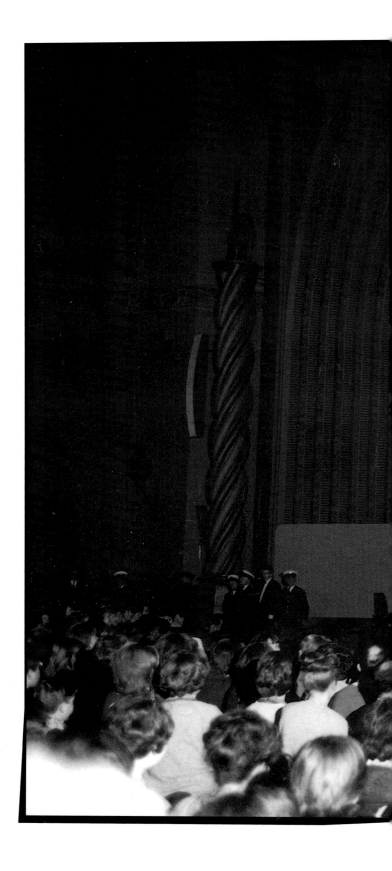

JELLY BABIES

A good seventy-five per cent of any Beatles audience at the time was made up of teenage girls. There were a few boys, who seemed to enjoy themselves, but they were very calm compared to the girls. The shot on the right is taken from the wings of the Astoria, Finsbury Park. Jelly babies, thrown by the fans, scatter the stage.

ALL TOGETHER

Different songs required different treatments, and John, Paul and George positioned themselves on stage accordingly. Here they cluster round one mike for 'I Wanna Hold Your Hand' and 'She Loves You'.

ON STAGE

*This is one of my favourite
on-stage shots of the Beatles,
taken at the Apollo, Manchester.
The fans seem to be enjoying
themselves, too.*

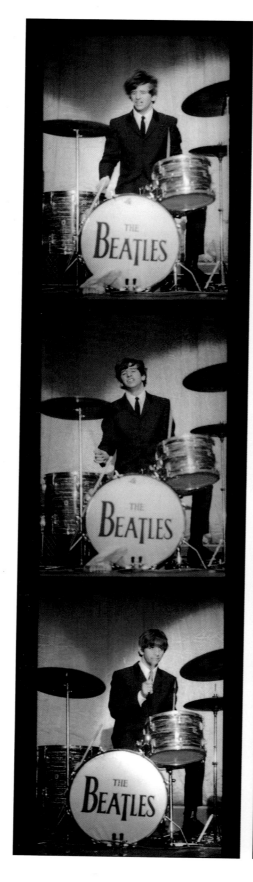
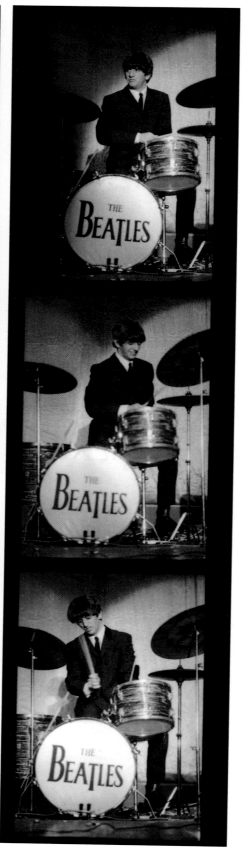

RHYTHM 'N' BLUES

Ringo joins in the vocals on 'She Loves You'. Later Ringo's idiosyncratic voice was heard singing lead on such tracks as 'Honey Don't' and 'Act Naturally'.

SHE LOVES YOU

*When two of the boys put their
heads together and hit the high
notes of 'She Loves You', it
invariably provoked a deafening
scream from the girls in the
audience.*

DUET

The fact that Paul played guitar left-handed made it easier for him to stand with his head close to John or George. This looked terrific and had a very powerful impact — it was as if they were singing to each other, and the fans loved it. Although John and George also sang with their heads together, it was not as effective as when either stood alongside Paul.

FINALE

The boys always ended their performance with a low bow to the audience. Even Ringo bows deeply from behind his drums.

it was thirty years ago today

4

KEEPING THE MADNESS AT BAY

Tight security surrounded the Beatles from the first day I met them. Arriving at the rather staid Branksome Towers, we had our first experience of the police protection that the Beatles had to have. Our press passes got us in, but the few fans who had also found their hide-out were being kept at bay by the men in blue at the end of the hotel's long driveway.

Well before a performance was due to start, the police would go on duty outside the theatre where the Beatles were to appear. Screaming teenage girls who had been unable to get tickets would be desperate for a glimpse of their idols, and the police had to be there to control the potential stampede. The Beatles themselves would either arrive hours early and be safely hidden in their dressing-room before the crowds gathered, or be smuggled in through a back door or side entrance.

The cost of all this police protection was enormous. Local councils began to ask themselves whether they could afford to allow the Beatles to perform in their town. Security arrangements were more costly than for those of royalty or top politicians.

UNDER SIEGE

Beatlemania comes to Bournemouth — a town normally dominated by retired gentlefolk and respectable holidaymakers. In the days before Bank Holiday hooliganism hit seaside resorts, the management of the Winter Gardens and the local police must have wondered what had hit them!

POLICE PROTECTION

*Once a performance was over, it
was back to the side entrance to
be hustled into a waiting police
van and whisked away. After the
Bournemouth show the van
delivered the boys to their
chauffeur-driven Austin Princess,
which took them back to their
hotel for a peaceful night.*

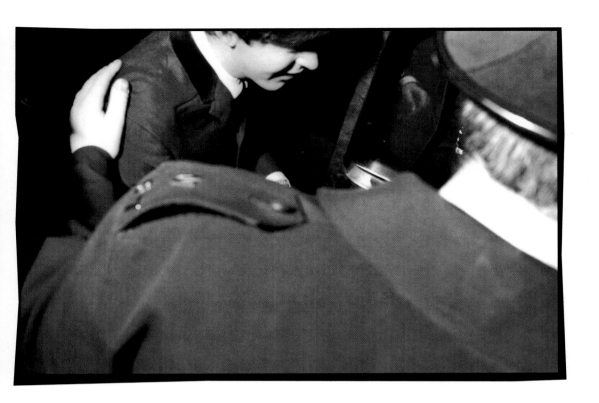

TWIST AND SHOUT AGAIN

Apparently unperturbed by the reaction they were provoking, the lads stamped and jerked rhythmically to the music. The girls went wild, and the Bournemouth constabulary only just managed to prevent the frenzied audience from storming the stage.

POLICE RELATIONS

The Beatles were easy-going and friendly with the police officers assigned to protect them, and developed a good-natured rivalry with some of them. One night at the Astoria three burly coppers lifted Ringo to the ceiling as he came off stage; he retaliated by showering them with torn-up pieces of paper: 'It's snowing!' he yelled. While the fans waited longingly at the stage door, their heroes indulged in a light-hearted free-for-all outside their dressing-room.

'It's For My Daughter'

Often the police officers themselves were fans — or had teenage daughters who would have killed to be where Mum or Dad were working — and getting the Fab Four's autographs was one of the perks of the job.

5

SHE LOVES YOU

That first night at the Winter Gardens was a bit of a culture shock for somebody who had recently been covering war stories in Africa. There were perhaps 3,000 people in the audience, at least 1,500 of them teenage girls. What with the shrill, frantic, almost orgasmic screams of the fans and the equally deafening megadecibel output of the huge amplifiers blaring out the beat, I thought the roof of the theatre would blow off.

Mayhem followed the Beatles wherever they went. Outside the theatre girls fought for a glimpse of them; inside, they screamed, cried, had hysterics. At the Apollo Theatre in Manchester, the chaos was such that Frank Allen climbed up a ladder before the show and installed two vast Ascor 600 strobe lights, flashing

back into the audience, so that I could photograph the fans' reactions. We also had powerful quartz iodine lamps and he found sockets for them, too. It was no mean achievement for Frank to keep the wires safe from stampeding feet. The management thought this extra lighting was all part of the show. I was able to stroll around on stage with a camera on a long lead, photographing the Beatles from behind, with the Ascors lighting up the whole theatre audience. People thought I was part of the show too!

Even though we recognised that the Beatles were something special, we couldn't believe this sort of enthusiasm would last.

We expected it all to die down in six months, eight months, a year perhaps. And so, we discovered, did the Beatles. When I first met them they were still just a group of Liverpool lads who had struck it lucky writing and performing music they loved.

NEVER TIRED OF WAITING

Fans used to wait for hours in the most awful weather for the Beatles to appear. They were almost always disappointed. When they eventually arrived at the London Palladium, overleaf, the boys were driven right up to the door and closely guarded by police as they dashed for the safety of the foyer.

THE BIRTH OF BEATLEMANIA

The girls used to fight to get on to the stage. I remember one girl in Manchester who was going simply crazy, leaping up out of her seat and tearing her hair. Whenever the attendants pushed her back she just popped up again like a jack-in-the-box — until a great burly policeman came up. I saw him lean over and say something to her, and then she sat down and stayed down. Afterwards I went up to him and asked, 'How did you do that?', to which he replied, 'I stood on her bloody toe — bloody hard!'

FAME

The Winter Gardens, Bournemouth, 16 November. This was the first time we met the Beatles and witnessed the scenes of hysteria that were becoming familiar all over the country.

SHE LOVES YOU

EXPIRING FANS

Fainting fans were commonplace, with bodies littering the foyer of the theatre. These scenes are at the Apollo in Manchester, where patients were tended by bemused St John's Ambulance and Red Cross volunteers. One nurse told me that some girls reached such peaks of excitement they genuinely had orgasms.

6

ON THE ROAD

The morning after we first met the Beatles, they were due to travel from their hotel outside Bournemouth to their next venue, the Coventry Theatre. They slept late, had breakfast in their rooms and escaped through the kitchen to their waiting limo. They invited me to join them while Frank followed in his car. We stopped en route at a small, unpretentious cafe – this was the only kind of place the boys could eat without being molested. Even so, waitresses of all ages and other customers came over to ask for their autographs, which they gave with smiles. Whenever I was with the Beatles they were always friendly and courteous with fans, and with anyone on tour who was there to help them.

After lunch their driver phoned ahead to the Coventry police to receive  instructions on where to rendezvous so that the Beatles could be escorted to the theatre safely. One of the police's requirements was that the boys be inside the theatre before 3.30 p.m., when the kids were let out of school. Nevertheless, there was a near riot as we arrived at the theatre and girls besieged the limo. The police hastily escorted the car away and the Beatles entered the theatre through a back door.

Their departure was even more dramatic, as they were whisked straight from the stage door to the limo. The doors were locked from the inside and the car sped away. This came to be a typical way to leave a show, though once at Portsmouth they escaped through an underground tunnel. On various occasions they borrowed policemen's helmets and overcoats or put on dark glasses and funny hats in an attempt to disguise themselves from the fans.

IN TRANSIT

*Outside the Branksome Towers
Hotel, near Bournemouth, where
Frank and I first met the Beatles.
Hotel staff and guests gathered
on the steps to wave the boys off
when they left for the Winter
Gardens, where they were to
perform that night. Even on the
way to a concert, Paul clutched
his ever-present transistor radio.*

SO WHICH ONE'S PAUL?

Wherever the Beatles went they could only eat at roadside cafes, because if they went anywhere more crowded, they'd be mobbed. The boys were always very friendly and willing to sign autographs for staff and customers alike. They didn't consider themselves great stars, too big for their public: on the contrary, they were normal, down-to-earth people.

7

THE FAB FOUR

So much has been written about the Beatles, both as a group and individually: John, the rebel with the devastatingly witty tongue; Paul, whose angelic choirboy looks hid a shrewd business brain; George, the gentleman, the serious one; Ringo, rather the odd one out, the perpetual clown – Beatles fans have been familiar with these rather glib summaries for the last thirty years.

Newspapers in the early 1960s were full of more or less ridiculous psycho-sociological comments about the Beatles and their popularity, but one that came close to my opinion said, 'It is the bubbly, uninhibited gaiety of the group that generates enthusiasm... They have an unforced individuality rather than a manufactured image.'

That was something Brian Epstein had recognised when he first saw them in the Cavern in Liverpool. Brought up on classical music, he thought their act was ragged and undisciplined and their clothes a mess – but 'I sensed at once there was something here. Something big. They must be groomed but remain untamed.'

Perhaps the best personal touch I can add is one provided by my daughter Cara. In November 1963 I took her along to an EMI photocall after the boys were awarded their first gold and silver discs. The Beatles knew all about her by now and greeted her warmly. Afterwards, as we left the building, Cara remarked to me, 'But Dad, they're so normal. Just ordinary boys.'

That's how I always felt about them, too.

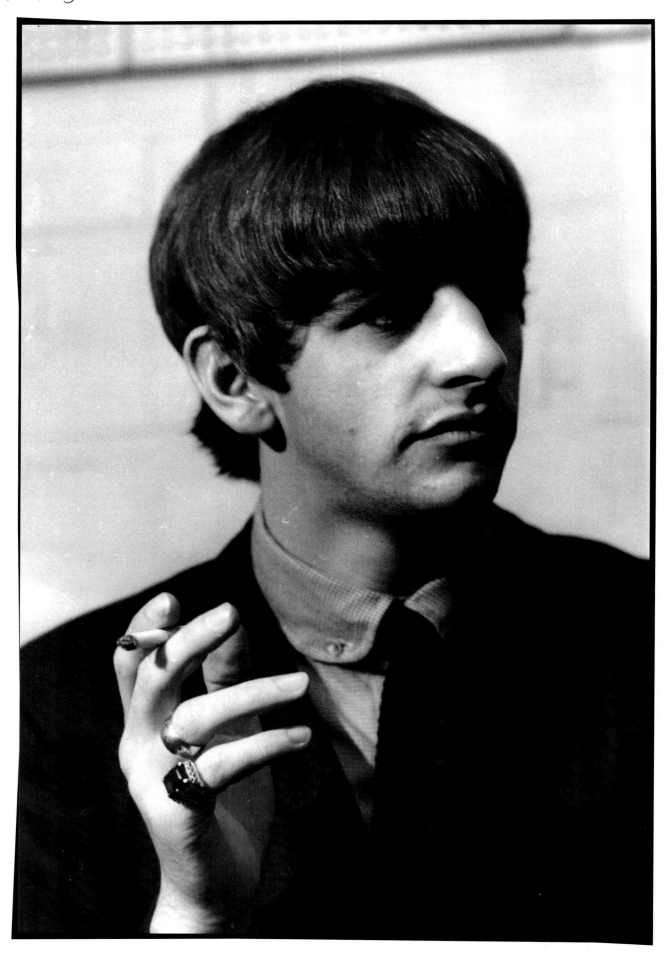

RINGO

When someone asked him why he wore so many rings on his fingers, he replied, 'Because I can't get them all through my nose.' Never the prime mover of the Beatles, he has been described as 'history's best remembered supporting player'. Perhaps because he was the outsider, he was able to take it all more calmly. Or perhaps, being Ringo, he just enjoyed himself while it lasted.

GEORGE

The quiet, polite one, always
slightly in Lennon's and
McCartney's shadows. Yet he and
John were the only ones to stay
friends after the Beatles broke up.
When John was killed, George
wrote a moving tribute to him
that included the line, 'You were
the one who invented it all'.
Nearly ten years later he had
some fun remembering those heady
days in a song called 'When We
Was Fab'.

it was thirty years ago today

PAUL

The day they met, Paul impressed John by his ability to tune a guitar and to remember the words of songs. Later, he explained to me how they wrote many of their songs: 'We would strum them out on our guitars and if, afterwards, we couldn't remember them, they weren't commercial … You can't lay down a formula for writing hits — why, if you could, you would found a great new industry.' Lennon and McCartney surely came close to doing just that.

JOHN

Always the wittiest of the group, he was also the most abrasive. 'People who think we had it easy can think again,' he said. 'Shortly before our big break, we had a good week when we made twenty pounds apiece and that was doing four shows a day.' He was also quite realistic about their position at the top: 'The day the fans desert us, I'll be wondering how to pay for my whisky and cokes. At the moment, we are at peak. Things can't get any more hysterical.' He was probably right, but he never did have to worry about who would pay the bills.

it was thirty years ago today

8
PLEASE, PLEASE ME

Although the Beatles and I got on well from the start, they obviously resented my constant presence at first. I suppose they felt I was invading their privacy. But as time went by they got used to my ever-clicking shutters; I started fading into the background and became part of the fittings. Looking back, I am surprised how few photographers I saw back stage with the Beatles, which was fortunate for *Life*. Also, only a few magazines were interested in in-depth coverage of pop groups in those days.

I had started my assignment in the face of considerable indifference from *Life*'s New York office. But late in 1963 the magazine's managing editor, George Hunt, had been driving into the city and was about to enter a tunnel when his teenage daughter shouted, 'Dad, stop the car! It's those fab Beatles on the radio! You know, Dad, this is the greatest ever pop group!'

In the office, George enquired of his foreign editor, 'Are we doing anything on the British Beatles?' 'Yes,' came the reply, 'we have Terry Spencer working on them.' That was true, but it had hardly been with his blessing!

However, the Beatles were about to make their first visit to the States and were due to appear on television on the Ed Sullivan Show, so George ordered us to go for a lead. Showbiz leads were rare in 1964. Our Beatles story filled eight pages of that prestigious magazine.

So suddenly *Life* wanted a cover. This had to be posed. We phoned Brian Epstein, who said he would arrange for the Beatles to be at the Astoria at least two hours before the start of their afternoon show. We had already seen how little control poor Brian had over the group, so we shouldn't have been surprised when they appeared only fifteen minutes before the curtain was due to go up. When our story ran in *Life* on 31 January 1964, the cover picture was of Geraldine Chaplin, fresh from her first stage success. The Beatles must be the only people in showbiz ever to have turned down a *Life* cover.

PHOTOCALL

An official EMI photocall in London. 'Serious' photographs of the Beatles always involved a lot of hanging around, drinking tea, getting bored and larking about. I much prefer these shots to the ones that were supposed to have been taken. The picture overleaf is one of the rare occasions when the boys actually posed for my camera — hardly a formal studio shot!

it was thirty years ago today

9

THE LOOK

When Brian Epstein first saw the Beatles their clothes were a mess, or so he thought. If they were to be successful, they had to smarten up.

They already had the Beatle haircuts that were to be copied by millions around the world. These were the brainchild of the German photographer Astrid Kirchherr, whom they had met when they were playing in Hamburg (she had

been engaged to the doomed 'fifth Beatle', Stu Sutcliffe). Brian allowed them to keep the mop-tops, but he made them discard the black leather John Lennon favoured (in Britain in the early sixties black leather still meant 'Nazi' to many people) and put them into lounge suits or, at worst, into matching polo-neck sweaters, tight black trousers and high-heeled boots. Tiny collars and lapels were fashionable, but it was the Beatles' collarless jackets that really caught on and became an intrinsic part of 'the look'.

With so many teenage girls madly in love with at least one of the Beatles, boys everywhere were forced into action. They may not have been able to write songs or play the guitar, but they could have a go at looking like these idols — and they did.

FROM TOP TO TOE

While girls everywhere were going wild about the Beatles' looks and sound, their brothers and boyfriends were queueing up to copy their style. Mop-tops, collarless jackets and high-heeled boots became the uniform of the fashion-conscious teenage boy.

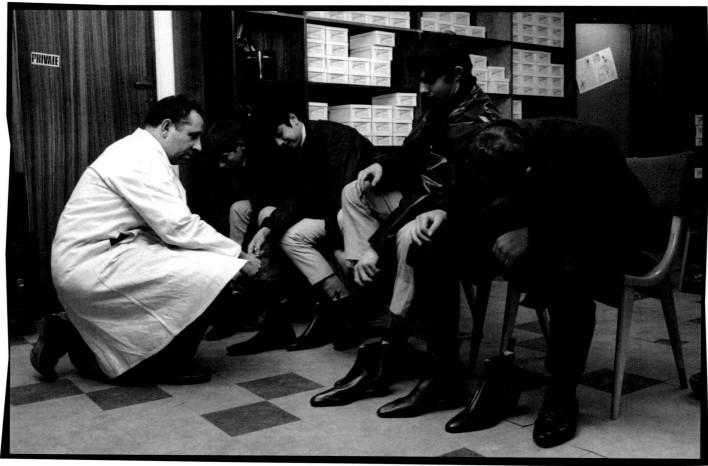

10

NICE TO SEE YOU

On 12 January 1964 the Beatles were booked to appear on Sunday Night at the London Palladium, a hugely popular television show hosted by Bruce Forsyth and broadcast live. It was their second appearance on the programme – the first, the previous autumn, had introduced a vast viewing public to Beatlemania for the first time. (In fact, it was after that show that a journalist coined the word.)

I had never seen the Beatles rehearse for any show, but for the January Palladium appearance they had been summoned for the whole of Sunday. It was a cold rainy day, yet the fans were outside in their hundreds. When the Beatles'

limo arrived it had to drive off again fast to avoid the screaming surge of girls. The boys transferred to two taxis and lay down on the floor in the back. The taxis arrived at the front entrance of the Palladium with their 'for hire' lights on, both doors flew open and the Beatles raced for the safety of the foyer.

Later in the afternoon, Tim Green, *Life* bureau chief in London, and I left by the stage door for something to eat. Passing a rubbish bin I picked up a liquorice allsorts carton and gave it to Tim. As a joke he called to the mob outside, 'Anyone want Ringo's liquorice packet?' He held it up. There was an almighty shriek as eight screaming girls descended on him and tore it out of his hand. If it had been one of the Beatles themselves, I imagine it could have turned nasty.

RELAXED REHEARSAL

Ringo and George sit in the stalls during the Palladium rehearsal and shoot pictures of other artists, previous page. Ringo became a keen photographer under my tuition!

This was the only occasion I ever saw the Beatles rehearsing, and even then they spent a lot of time fooling about.

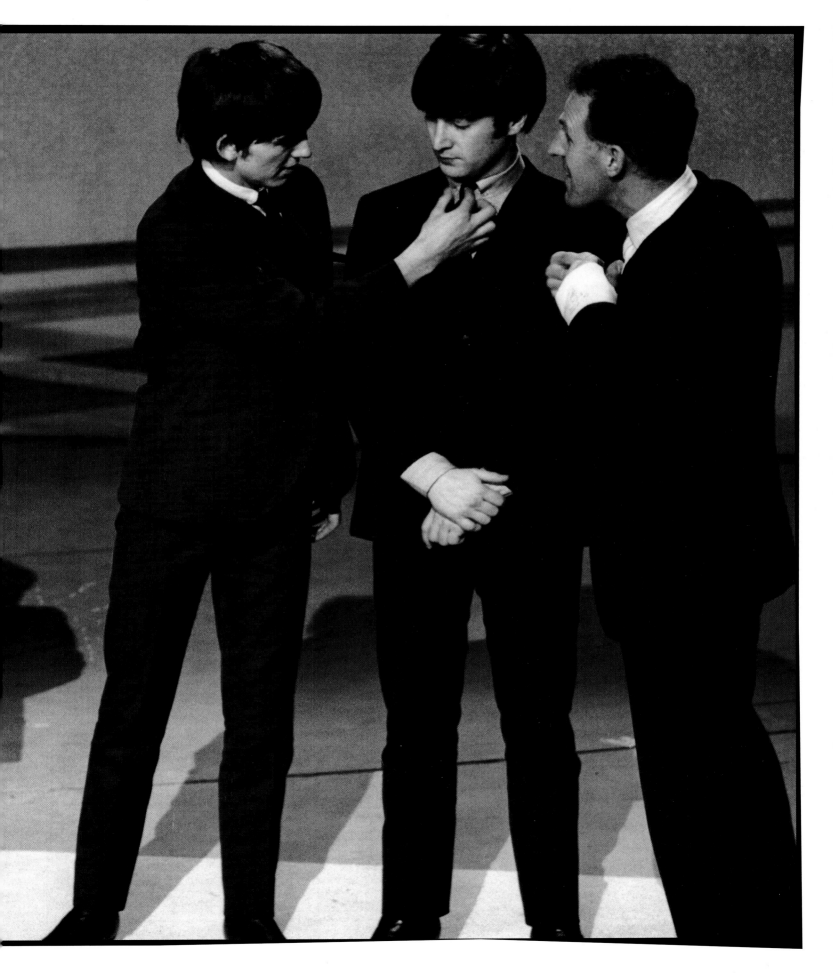

WITH THE BOSS

This picture (top left) shows Brian Epstein with the Beatles at the rehearsal; Neil Aspinall, the Beatles' road manager, stands behind.

SUBTITLES

Refusing to be serious even about appearing live on television in one of the most popular shows of the week, the Beatles poke fun at compere Bruce Forsyth during rehearsal. Bruce had invited them to appear on a future programme, but the boys were booked to fly to Paris next day.

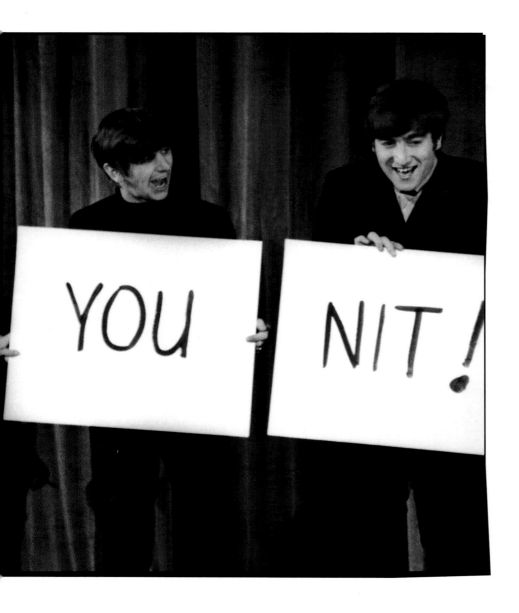

SUNDAY NIGHT AT THE PALLADIUM

On stage at the Palladium with other members of the cast. The Beatles' friend Alma Cogan (in the black dress) appeared on the same show.

11
PARIS

The day after they appeared on Sunday Night at the London Palladium, the Beatles flew to Paris for a three-week engagement at L'Olympia. In these days of international travel it is hard to imagine what a big event this was. The Beatles had been to Hamburg several years earlier, but they were still struggling young rockers then, travelling by road in a battered minibus, playing late-night shows in

dingy clubs and sleeping irregular hours in squalid digs. Now they were stars, topping a bill that included local girl Sylvie Vartan and the American Trini Lopez, fresh from a big hit in the UK with 'If I Had a Hammer'. Crowds massed at Heathrow to see three of their heroes off on their first big foreign trip; Ringo was fogbound in Liverpool, though he was also reported to be unhappy about something and threatening not to go.

Brian Epstein, always one for the grand gesture, had booked not only himself and the boys but their entire entourage into one of Paris's top hotels, the Georges Cinq. Despite the pre-publicity, Beatlemania had not yet reached France and the boys were free to wander about the streets, seeing the sights of Paris, only occasionally being recognised and asked for an autograph. There was a small police presence at the hotel, but the only disruption I saw was back stage at L'Olympia – and it was caused not by the fans but by the paparazzi, desperate to get a shot of the boys. They threatened to break down the dressing-room door, but were quickly dispersed by hastily summoned gendarmes.

INCONSPICUOUS

After their months of virtual imprisonment at home, it was a great relief for the Beatles to be able to walk the streets of Paris unmolested. They particularly asked me to be unobtrusive in my photo-taking so as not to draw attention to them. A very few people recognised them and asked for autographs. As always, the Beatles were polite and friendly, trying out their minimal French on the fans: 'Merci bucup' was about their limit.

Brian Sommerville, the Beatles' press officer, can be seen with Paul below.

TRAVELLING IN STYLE

Although the Beatles had flown to Paris, their driver and Austin Princess had come across too. Here, all four of the boys are crammed into the back seat of the limo as a French photographer grabs a shot of them.

it was thirty years ago today

TAKE TWO

Having failed to take a cover picture at the Astoria, I persuaded the Beatles to come to the Eiffel Tower and try again. Alas, the tower was enshrouded in mist.

The picture overleaf shows the Beatles accompanied by Brian Sommerville and Mal Evans, their road manager (in the background).

THE COOL FRENCH

Beatlemania had yet to hit Paris. The only excitement was among the photographers back stage — the elegant first-night audience remained calm and gave the boys a lukewarm reception. The following morning's papers suggested that Trini Lopez was the real star of the show.

OÙ SONT LES GENDARMES?

An elaborate display in an uncrowded foyer was in contrast to the hysterical crowds at the Beatles' performances in Britain. Similarly the audience stayed in their seats and there was no need for policemen.

12

EPSTEIN'S EMPIRE

Brian Epstein was several years older than the Beatles; Jewish, middle-class, privately educated, with an interest in classical music, he seemed an odd choice for the Beatles' manager. In fact, it was Brian who had chosen them.

Brian's father owned a thriving electrical business in Liverpool, including a shop called NEMS (North End Music Stores), where Brian ran the record department. One Saturday in October 1961 several customers came into his shop to ask for a record by a new group called the Beatles. (The record, strangely enough, was the old folk song 'My Bonnie Lies Over the Ocean', which the Beatles had released on the advice of their record company, Polydor.) Brian had never heard of the Beatles and was amazed to find that they were playing in the Cavern Club, literally a few minutes' walk away from the NEMS shop. He went to see them, was overwhelmed, and became their manager within weeks.

A complete perfectionist, Brian was great for the Beatles at the start. But he took on too much. Six months after signing up the Beatles, he was also looking after Gerry and the Pacemakers, and he later added Cilla Black, Billy J. Kramer, the Dakotas and others to the list. His meticulousness also made him a bad delegator: when the Beatles' career took off, in a way that nobody could have predicted, he couldn't cope. He had no control over the lads' actions and he had his own problems. Charming and amazingly successful, he still never quite fitted in.

Yet without him, the Beatles might never have made the break from lunchtime concerts at the Cavern. The world owes Brian Epstein a great deal.

ADVICE UNHEEDED

Brian lived in the forlorn hope of getting the Beatles to toe the line. He was always giving them earnest advice, or encouraging them to listen to instructions. But although he arranged the bookings and dealt with the money, he had little control over their behaviour.

NUMBER 1

Gerry and the Pacemakers hit the Number 1 spot in early 1963, before the Beatles had managed that feat. (In fact, Gerry and the Pacemakers' first three records were to make it to Number 1, an achievement that remained unmatched for twenty years.) There was an understandable amount of friendly rivalry within Brian Epstein's 'stable'.

Gerry Marsden can be seen with a fan on the right.

SUCCESS STORIES

*The rest of Epstein's empire, with
Tommy Quickly, Cilla and Billy
J. Kramer to the fore; Sounds Inc.
and The Fourmost stand behind.
Brian, as so often, looks a little
uncomfortable.*

MANAGEMENT TEAM

Brian Epstein and his P.A., Derek Taylor, enjoy Cilla's success on television. According to Gerry Marsden, Brian had a clear vision of the future for his protégés. By this time the Beatles' extraordinary success was assured, but Brian correctly envisaged Gerry appearing in stage musicals and forecast that Cilla would triumph as a 'personality'.

ANYONE WHO HAD A HEART

Brian Epstein and Derek Taylor study a press article about Cilla Black, pictured right with Tommy Quickly, Epstein and Billy J. Kramer (left to right).

13

UNACCUSTOMED AS I AM

Beatles records were in the charts for sixty-eight weeks of 1963, sixteen of them at Number 1, and for seventy-two weeks in 1964, with twelve at Number 1. These achievements were not unique, but they were still phenomenal. Nobody in the history of the pop charts has had more Number 1 hits and only Elvis Presley has spent more weeks at the top. By the end of 1964 the Beatles had topped popularity polls all over the English-speaking world and were also beginning to make their impact elsewhere.

No other pop stars had ever become so accepted by the establishment. To be awarded silver and gold discs is the privilege of any successful recording artist; to top popularity polls means gaining the affection of the kids, the target audience. But to be invited to private receptions at Australia House, to be presented to royalty — at the time, this was practically unheard of for rock musicians.

The ultimate establishment accolade came in the Queen's Birthday Honours List of 1965 when the Beatles were awarded the MBE. Although some former recipients of the award sent it back in disgust, most of the younger generation were delighted to see their heroes justly rewarded. If the award was, as many have suggested, a popularity-courting move on the part of Prime Minister Harold Wilson, it was certainly a successful one.

CELEBRATIONS

On 18 November 1963 EMI, the Beatles' record company, gave a party in London to present them with their first gold and silver discs for 'Please, please me'. EMI Chairman Sir Joseph Lockwood (on the left) made the presentations. My daughter Cara met the Beatles on this occasion: they were charming to her, despite what her father was doing to them, and she, devoted fan though she was, was struck by how normal they were.

Gerald Marks, managing editor of Disc Weekly, also enjoys their success (bottom left). Epstein can be seen in the background.

AUSTRALIA HOUSE

*In April 1964 the Beatles had the
top six records in a local chart in
Sydney and the boys were invited
to a reception at Australia House.
George is warmly welcomed by
Prime Minister Robert Menzies.*

IN THE WINGS

The annual New Musical Express awards ceremony at the Empire Pool, Wembley, for winners of the paper's readers' polls. Brian sits in the wings watching the boys perform.

14

IN HIS OWN WRITE

John had always been a bit of an artist and a poet. He used to scribble away in a notebook at school and continued to do so whenever he had the chance in dressing-rooms or on the road. In early 1964 he published a collection of his drawings and verse under the title *John Lennon: In His Own Write*. It was the first public sign that he wanted to do things away from the group, that just being a Beatle was not enough.

The bookshop Foyle's honoured the publication with a literary luncheon, held on 23 April at the Dorchester Hotel. The chairman was Osbert Lancaster, and guests included such showbiz luminaries as Arthur Askey, Harry Secombe, Millicent Martin and Joan Littlewood. Fellow pop stars Helen Shapiro and Marty Wilde were there, as were Yehudi Menuhin, Victor Silvester, Mary Quant and the cartoonist Giles. Members of the public could attend on payment of twenty-one shillings. Strangely, none of the other Beatles was present, though Brian Epstein, of course, was.

Osbert Lancaster's speech included this tribute to the Beatles: 'In the Royal Variety Show they shone out like a good deed in a naughty world. They have established something pretty rare, something which has the same measure of success as the old English music hall — an accord between the stage and the audience. They represent, however different their methods may be, the genuine strength in English entertainment far more successfully than rows of ladies and gentlemen tramping about with bustles and false whiskers.'

John, in reply, said merely, 'Thank you very much, and God bless you.'

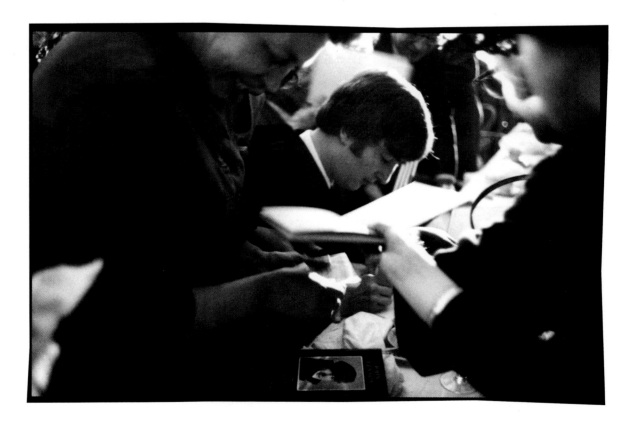

SIGNING SESSION

Crowds queue in Foyle's for signed
copies of In His Own Write.

LUNCH WITH FOYLE'S

The Foyle's luncheon: John arrives with his then wife Cynthia. Wilfrid Brambell, who had recently appeared as Paul's grandfather in A Hard Day's Night, *sits on Cynthia's right; Marty Wilde and Harry Secombe are on her left.*

MR AND MRS LENNON

Cynthia and John with Victor Spinetti.

A FELLOW PROFESSIONAL
*Brian charms Christina Foyle
(top) and signs his autograph,
while luncheon chairman and
fellow cartoonist Osbert Lancaster
seems less delighted with John's
company.*

SIXTIES GLITTERATI

Another guest of honour was Lionel Bart, the toast of London and Broadway for his success with Oliver! *His new musical,* Maggie May, *was about to hit the West End.*

222

AND IN THE END...

And what about thirty years on? There are still three Beatles, now in their fifties, and legends in their own lifetimes. One of them, Paul McCartney, is certainly one of the richest men in show business.

The murder of John Lennon in New York was a terrible shock to me, even though I knew him only peripherally. After the early association with the Beatles in the sixties I lost touch with them, but I still listen to their music and certainly have not lost the memories of those old exciting days.

How great it is for me thirty years later to see negatives which have lain around my photo library burst forth into this superb book. Thanks to the 'eye' and art of Roy Williams.

I had nothing to do with the vision of this book: that vision goes entirely to David Reynolds and Penny Phillips at Bloomsbury.

Terence Spencer, 1994